MUSICOLEPSY

MUSICOLEPSY

Jonathan Taylor

Printed by imprintdigital
Upton Pyne, Exeter
www.imprintdigital.net

Typeset by types of light
typesoflight@gmail.com

Published by Shoestring Press
19 Devonshire Avenue, Beeston, Nottingham, NG9 1BS
(0115) 925 1827
www.shoestringpress.co.uk

First published 2013

ISBN 978-1-907356-72-8

ACKNOWLEDGEMENTS

Versions of the following poems have appeared in or on the following magazines, books, webzines, radio stations and websites: *Acumen, Agenda, Ambriel Revolution, And Other Poems, The Aesthetica*, BBC Radio 3, *Connotation Press: An Online Artifact, Crrritic!*, ed. John Schad and Oliver Tearle (Eastbourne: Sussex Academic Press, 2011), *Envoi, Great River Review, Hearing Voices, Indent, Ink, Sweat & Tears, The Interpreter's House, Iota, LeftLion, The London Magazine, The London Miscellany, Men in the Company of Women*, ed. Apryl Skies and Alicia Winski (Sherman Oaks: Edgar & Lenore Publishing, 2013), N.A.S.A.-Chandra X-ray Observatory, *New Trespass, New Walk, Platinum Page, Poetic Diversity, Poetry Cornwall, Poetry Scotland, The Seventh Quarry, Spilt Milk, Stand, Staple*. Thanks are due to all the editors involved.

Thanks are also due to staff and students at De Montfort University, particularly Kathleen Bell, Will Buckingham, Simon Perril and Phil Cox; to John Lucas for his kind and wise guidance; and with love to my father, my mother, Robin, Anna, Sam, Naomi, Erin, Karen, Bruce, Finola, Tancred, Helen, Ben, Dylan, and, of course, Maria, Miranda and Rosalind. The E. T. A. Hoffmann epigraph is from 'Automata,' trans. Major Alexander Ewing, in *The Best Tales of Hoffmann*, ed. E. F. Bleiler (New York: Dover, 1967), pp. 71–103, 97. Courtesy of Dover Publications Inc. All rights reserved. The epigraph to 'György Ligeti, Poème Symphonique for 100 Metronomes' is from Alfred Schnittke, *A Schnittke Reader*, ed. Alexander Ivashkin, trans. John Goodliffe (Bloomington & Indianapolis: Indiana University Press, 2002), p. 225. Courtesy of Indiana University Press. All rights reserved.

CONTENTS

For Maria

There has come down to us ... that beautiful notion of the Music of the Spheres.... Can the music which dwells within us be any other than that which lies buried in nature as a profound mystery, comprehensible only by the inner, higher sense?

– E.T.A. Hoffmann, 'Automata'

EXPOSITION DU SYSTÈME DU MONDE

My daughter's blah-blah babbles coalesce
into proto-words, "hiyas" and "mamas"
condensing from the nebular static,
planetesimals among the diffuse
molecular cloud

                sucked inwards over
what must seem to her millions of years
by gravity towards a centre round which –
as if she were acting out Laplace's
equations – particles spin towards
one another,

                an accretion leading to
planets and moons locked in a *mécanique*
céleste, which might seem a clockwork, rule-bound
equilibrium,

                till you remember
the comets, their tails like poetry.

!!**&@??

After N.A.S.A.-Chandra X-ray Observatory,
'A Cosmic Exclamation Point,' 11 August 2011.

In the beginning was the Word, and the Word was with God.

– John, 1

302 in *Arp's Atlas of Peculiar Galaxies*
is UGC-9618, 450 million
light years away in Boötes constellation,
plunging shard VV340 North
piercing spiral eye VV340 South,
its million years of shrieking and shock
expressed as infrared exclamation mark,

in a night sky light-years-full of cosmic
punctu-radi-ation: stars asterisks,
Saturn in parenthesis, comets dashes,
binaries colons or semi-colons
depending on relative masses,
Horsehead Nebula a question,
black holes full-stops in gravitation,
Arp's gallery of galaxies
ampersands, dittos, obeli, ellipses –

and a typo-cosmographist might decipher
the universe as a Word under erasure,
a daring act
                    of apocalyptic swearing.

BLACK HOLE IN B-FLAT

Astronomers using N.A.S.A.'s Chandra X-ray Observatory have found, for the first time, sound waves from a supermassive black hole....

– N.A.S.A.-Chandra, 9 September 2003

For 2.5 billion years you've groaned,
B-flat 57 octaves below middle-C.

For 2.5 billion years you've moaned
for no-one, because no-one
could hear you from Perseus Cluster
250 million light years away,
your galactic ground-bass a million billion
times lower than human hearing,
dog hearing, even Keplerian hearing,

who would have been hard pushed
to retain an equal temperament
in the face of such monotony –
more monkish medieval drone
than planetary polyphony,

as if Palestrina never happened,
and Bach dozed off at the organ
shortly after the Big Bang,
his elbow resting on a pedal point
over which he dreamt his flickering fugues,
short-lived as novas,
       short-lived as life,
            short-lived as anything but you,
              and all-too-soon
                  sucked back down
                     into your B-flat abyss.

CATALOGUE DES NÉBULEUSES ET DES AMAS D'ÉTOILES

A supernova remnant
Four planetary nebulae
Six diffuse nebulae
Twenty-seven star clusters
Twenty-seven spiral galaxies
Four lenticular galaxies
Eight elliptical galaxies
And one irregular galaxy:

Messier 1: Crab Nebula
Messier 6: Butterfly Cluster
Messier 8: Lagoon Nebula
Messier 17: Swan Nebula
Messier 20: Trifid Nebula
Messier 24: Sagittarius Star Cloud
Messier 33: Triangulum Galaxy
Messier 51: Whirlpool Galaxy
Messier 63: Sunflower Galaxy

all first chronicled out of irritability
by eighteenth-century astronomer
and comet-hunter Charles Messier

as a reverse-map of what to ignore,
which deep-sky efflorescences,
rainbowed light-years of space
might be disregarded, blinked at,
because they got in the way
of the astronomical fame
of observing a new comet.

His catalogue, nebulae and Trifids,
Crabs, clusters and Butterflies,
Sunflowers, Lagoons and galaxies

survived him.

HISTORY LESSON

N.A.S.A.'s Chandra X-ray Observatory has found a cosmic 'ghost' lurking around a distant supermassive black hole.

– N.A.S.A.-Chandra, 28 May 2009

Telescoped, the universe is a vast memory,
an over-long school-lesson in cosmic history,
background radiation droning on and on
from 300,000 years after the big bang,
remembering anything big enough (not us);

black-holes are hangover-haunted by X-ray fuzz,
groaning about binges on long-ago nights
which climaxed in billions of star-bursts of vomit
heaving energy across light-years of galaxy,
as if these mouths had consumed something too spicy;

supernovae remember how they first happened,
old men reminiscing in star-remnants' patterns
about halcyon days when they were suns too,
until thermonuclear dementia tore through
their molten synapses

               – and we know that
when any-sun forgets so much is lost, past,
local light-years of knowledge, years in the million,
till nothing is left except a history of billions.

THERMODYNAMIC EQUILIBRIUM

You knew your laws of thermodynamics:

that energy transfers from hotter bodies
to colder ones – a process not
spontaneously reversible;

so perhaps you knew too that

it'd only be after 10^{100} years
or thereabouts, following the dark era
of leptons and photons hanging out,

it'd only be in that final heat death
of maximum entropy, when
microstasis equals macrostasis

and nothing, no stars, no planets,
no graves can happen any longer
forever and ever and ever,

only then would we again
be the same temperature,
and $S = k.\ log\ W$ –

where entropy (S)
is Boltzmann constant (k)
times the natural logarithm of microstates
consistent with macrostate (W) –

will no longer pertain.

CINE-CAMERA

We walk about, amid the destinies of our world-existence, encompassed by
dim but ever present Memories of a Destiny more vast – very distant in the
bygone time, and infinitely awful.

– Edgar Allan Poe, Eureka

Cine-cameraing backwards,
that was what we demanded
on those projected afternoons,
as forward history was consumed

by a flickering bluish flame
imposed on our childish games
like some retrospective truth;
but we craved comedy not combustion,

and at ten it was always amusing
to see slides un-sliding,
sandcastles untrampling,
father's faces unlining,

leavings un-waving –
and I thought the back-spooling
might undo forever
if father were distracted from projector,

forgetting the off-switch,
before the first cartridge,
re-embryoing the family,
Super-8 de-historied –

then faster, wars parting like seas,
flattened empires arising like soufflés,
apes gladly unshackled
from learning, dinosaurs slinking back

to the sea, fish consumed by fires –
then faster still, systems, stars
sucking in cheeks with pop and crackle,
tracing the way home, in a borealitic smile

13.7 billion years long,
where the film almost comes
to a halt, what is left of the universe
coyly pin-pirouetting in slow reverse

through its last million years
and coalescing lakes of quark tears
to the final 10^{-6} of a second,
slowing almost to the point of points,

that pre-Planck moment,
when density, temperature were infinite,
and encased in prismatic rainbows
were all laws, histories, camera frames,

and we – supernovae, black holes, galaxies,
slid slides, crushed sandcastles –
merely the epiphenomenon
of that first shattering, that blue flaming.

MONTSERRAT

This day is a victory: it wavers already, it flees, the Spirit of Gravity, my old arch-enemy.

— Friedrich Nietzsche, *Thus Spake Zarathustra*

The film ends in an upside-down monastery,
Montserrat, the Abbey of Santa Maria,
dropped camera die-dreaming beyond gravity,
4,055 feet underneath Catalonia.

The Benedictines are inverted pyramids
on serrated floor of Miranda de les Agulles,
Sant Jeroni, Montgrós, and, according to legends,
always out of shot, a levitating Holy Grail.

Those I know, just before the film burns out,
I see standing on heads; only their mumbled words
defy reverse gravity, so they can't be made out,
falling into the sun, like goodbyes unheard.

FOR MY FATHER

... but Purcell's Dido's lament –

When I am laid in earth,
May my wrongs create
No trouble in thy breast;
Remember me, but ah! forget my fate

– never seems to finish,
and the five-bar *basso ostinato*
recurs again and again,
closing like a trap on the Carthage Queen,
remembering what she wants forgotten,
the 3/2 rhythm persisting
long after the record has finished,
chaconning my footsteps
towards the C.D. player
and the Eject button,

which can't eject the *ostinato*
from my head and can't stop me
remembering the Queen's fate
encased within it –
the slit wrists, the betrayal,
all that *Aeneid* balls-up –

and I know what the circling *ostinato* tells me:
that despite those seven last words
her fate is to be remembered for her fate,
to be immortalised for nothing else;

and I know too that grief,
the ground-bass to all our memories,
all too often memorialises by mistake
the fate, the last illness, the how
and not the who or what.

CARS

Sleepless anxiety has shrunk it all,
paranoia, Parkinson's, dementia, Capgras,
into a twenty-five-year-old matchbox
long before any kind of diagnosis,
but after I'd stopped vrooming my cars
every £1 of which was bought for me
by my father on Saturdays over years
from Smith's in Newcastle as a treat
"for being a good boy," or pretending to be.
Another car-dealing boy who wasn't good
asked me to give them to him in charity.
I no longer needed them so he felt I should
trade in my vans, lorries, planes and diggers.
My father's face was die-cast when I told him
I could never get them or, for that matter,
those W. H. Smith's afternoons back again.

CAKE CASE

i.m. M. K., d. Torquay, 2001

The disease microscoped
the E.coli of your fury
which had been breeding
for decades in a prison-mess
awaiting its moment of release.

With microscope inverted
outer kitchen seemed diminished,
indirectly proportional to bacterial rage,

as your famed cooking & caking
was Model-Village-ised
by half-millimetres, icily baroqued,

your fairies anorexic,
rocks igneous, ashy,
butterflies dispersed on Devonshire gales,
Easter nests of Dodos
          lopsided & sinking
                    into a chocolate fossilisation.

Meanwhile main courses
were all but mislaid,
stranded & Sundayed
on decrusted bread,
tongue quarter-sandwiches
sliced tremblingly

thinner than sanity.

HOW LONG IS THE COASTLINE OF BRITAIN?

i.m. Benoît Mandelbrot (1924-2010)

The coastline is doilyed
with snowflakes on snowflakes,
crystalline equations on equations
according to paradox

$$L(G) = MG^{1-D}$$

where coastal length (L) is function
of measurement scale (G) *ad infinitum*,

inlets, estuaries, headlands
on headlands, estuaries, inlets
fractalically blizzarding
under impossible microscopes

into icy,
sub-atomic

geo-

me-

try.

MAJORCA, 2006

Over the top of Austen I see them:
transporting wheelchair to water's edge,
lifting him by armpits into the surge,
supporting his neck, his legs, his back
sometimes chatting, sometimes distracted –
splashing, batting balls, ducking, shouting –
grandparents, parents, friends, siblings
ranged like rings round a distant planet
which to outsiders might seem icy, silent.
I hear the father say to a friend in passing:
"Yes, it was a shame," while still beaming.

I recline my sunbed, readjust sunglasses,
sip my cocktail, flick through pages,
on these between-days feeling orbitless.

THE CHASMS, ISLE OF MAN

Such were the joys,
When we all girls & boys…

– William Blake, 'The Ecchoing Green'

On unbeachy days, they brought the children here:
past the derelict house chalked CHASMS,
where the world's end cries into oceans,
tear after sandstone tear.

Down from the half-house warning CHASMS,
through heath, hawthorn, ears-full of sleet,
to where gulls cried far beneath their feet,
marched Robins, Jonathans, Karens.

Through heath, hawthorn, micro-gales,
leaping over fissures bound together
only by cobwebs, spiders and heather
and an orphan pebble falls and fails

to splash, jumping 400-foot fissures,
daring the cliff-edge, never reaching it,
children would play till chasms brimmed with night,
ruptured by avalanchine sorrows –

turning from that cliff-edge they never reached,
leaving the island's graveside,
leaving these ancient tombstones of quartzite
for a human tomorrow, more beachy,

but for the isle's graveside these girls and boys,
these children were a split second of joy,
now alone with forty million years of weeping to go,
an inhuman tomorrow and tomorrow and tomorrow.

PLANET WALK, GRANADA ARBORETUM, JODRELL BANK

Each step took us ten million kilometres
from one another,

gravitation's inverse-square law
affecting us too

as we drifted from the dish of Lovell
and our Sun's pull,

scouring outer reaches of Solar System's
Autumnal arboretum

for far-flung planets Uranus and Neptune,
where we started losing

one another round hawthorn, past crabapples
large as Jupiter's spot,

mountain ash hung with galaxies of berries,
nebulae of heather,

till alone I called from overgrown meadow
that I'd discovered Pluto

but gravity there is a fifteenth of Earth's own,
so no-one came.

STERILE PROMONTORY, JULY 1982

Ankle-deep in New Brighton
beach, yellow kagools
greyed by drizzle, ears
shrill-sopranoed by the
coloratura westerly,
reminded – as if we needed
reminding, coming from
where we came from –
that childhood is not
one long summer but
one long preparation
for something colder,
greyer, drizzlier,
sinking into a mini-spit
of squelchy sand,
corrugated, cobbled
by northern waves,
we worry round and round
hundreds of white crabs –
in limp lieu of Blackpool's
arcade games, or Southport's
spiky grass wars –
until their legs fall off,
trying and failing
to reanimate them with driftwood,
but this beach is the opposite
of a crustacean Revelations,
as salt puddle graves
suck back their dead,

while my crabby father keeps
hearing (in his head)
the Last Trump, which is the
station tannoy announcing
the Last Train. He's been
as worried as the crabs
about the train back
since we got the train here,
look-look-looking at his watch,
in case we get too engrossed
with crab corpses
and miss the train, miss home,
miss everything.

We're here at the end
of a fourteen-day rover ticket:
fourteen days out,
but we've run out
of Blackpools, Southports,
Holyheads, even Morecambes,
and are reduced to this,
a northern charlatan
for something better
we've never seen,
which looks older than the
older original –
Martin Parr's *Last Resort*.

But looking through his photos,
I remember none of it:
not the ice-cream-drizzled
faces, nor the fish-and-chip
melée, nor the concrete
sand-castles

and for me
New Brighton has shrunk
to this crabby promontory
of eroding sand-mud memory,
surrounded by incoming tides
and the miniature, eddying dead.

CASSETTE

Thus a £1.99 cassette remembers voices
which are different from those in my head,
my father higher, more tenor-Lancastrian:
"No second chances,"
         "It was Daniel in the Den,"
my brother and sister more Stoke-on-Trent:
"Etna, Mauna Kea,"
         "Her bite wrecked my shot,"
my younger sister shrill-proto-techno:
"Me need toilet-toilet, toilet-toilet, now-now."
"A good one's Kilimanjaro," my father says.

There are snooker pauses and clinks,
recorded evidence of Karen's cheating
who moves black while no-one's looking
because as always Robin's winning.
Helen's beneath the table all toys and teeth
and I'm voiceless next door in the kitchen,
homeworking volcanic eruptions
with my mother whose questions
pour like lava through the cubby-hole:
"He wants one you can walk up?"

Omnipresent father answers, "Vesuvius,"
while adjudicating black-ball disputes
and fuzzy-felt Biblical tableaux
in which Darius's lions devour Noah
in a topsy-turvy Garden of Gethsemane.

But in the cassette's magnetic garden
no Judas will kiss-betray us to the future
for the tape would hardly recognise
my memory's recorded echoes
believing till it snaps that nothing it knows
will ever change

                    apart from my sister
who gives up cheating at snooker
to start practising piano scales instead.

THINGS MY BROTHER AND SISTER TAUGHT ME

That Brazil is the capital of Europe
That triangles have six right angles
That babies come from sharing soap
That rows caused by winning games
were never worth the bother

That schools dance on taxi bonnets
in New York, never Stoke-unfamous-Trent

That, born here, we won't live forever.

JOSIAH WEDGWOOD (1730-95)

All is in retrospect...

– Katherine Mansfield, *Letters*

And there's his likeness: 'Vase-Maker General
to the Universe,'
               master of misnamed Etruria,
frock-coated, bewigged, buckled and breeched
in bronze, not porcelain, decorpsed, brushed down
and statued since 1863,

faux-Portland Vase
               – a copy of his copies,
made for Jasperware gentries,
                   speaking
Enlightenment Greek on mantelpieces,
chiming sugared slave-songs when stirred –

aloft in one hand, a student's empty Foster's
in the other, as if now, alone, as Etruria
is taken over
               not by Romans
but new imitators,
               new creditors,

he's retrospectively weighing up options.

ON STOKE STATION, SATURDAY 18TH NOVEMBER 2000, 5.50PM

Everything on the station was to blame, it seemed,
for the giant-killing by Nuneaton Borough AFC
who had scored in the ninetieth minute,
though I'd no idea when I stepped right into it.

Home fans wouldn't let the fiasco end there
so Potters had chased the non-leaguers here
all the way from the Britannia Stadium.

Even the phone box was fifth columnist
and I watched it shatter amid the scrambling
so no-one outside Stoke could call in
to hear about F. A. Cup failure or vice versa.

Outside Stoke, though, was still in my ears –
on my personal stereo, of all things, *Star Wars*
which seemed to choreograph rioters around me,
who swore with kitsch Hollywood melodies,
wielded baseball bats gracefully as light sabres

and I, C-3PO, walked straight through the lasers,
against the march of Stormtroopers and panic
to a taxi, untouched, protected by naff music.

RECORD SHOP, LIME STREET, LIVERPOOL

i.m. Auntie Mildred

Their accents were a different r.p.m. to my Potteries
so it took me a while to understand that their row
wasn't an operatic prelude to a fight but was about
whose Mahler Five was best, Bernstein's or Barbirolli's,

one maintaining the latter was too flaccid, *Mancunian*,
another accusing the flamboyant New Yorker
of trans-Atlantic showmanship. It really mattered
and unbathed mates on pensions and benefits joined in.

I picked my way through the rubble of orchestral L.P.s,
thinking of my aunties in '30s terraced slums
hungrily reading Shakespeare and Dickens,
thankful the shop wasn't a front for gangsters, thieves.

When I found my way back, many years later,
the shop had been crushed under the station eaves.
As if out of a general sense of disbelief
snobbish bulldozers had cleared this street of Mahler.

OUR PRICE, 1995

Music ... makes one feel part of one whole, which one loves all alike, losing the sense of a separate self.

— George Eliot

I worked there once for a few months till Christmas
alienated from its music, loudspeakers, Pulp, Oasis
and especially the queues for Robson and Jerome.
I whistled Mozart, mind's ear on my stereo at home.

I couldn't find my way round chart or back catalogue,
directed to Tesco's people who asked for Suggs,
gave customers the wrong Simon, Paul not Carly,
grimaced when sent to look under Nail, Jimmy.

I blamed my amygdala, frontal lobes, myelination
coating my axons, petrifying my dispositions,
but un-neurological colleagues who didn't see this
pushed me into shelves, made me clear up the mess.

As I was tidying, a posh lady came to the counter,
asked for the *Magic Flute* with a particular conductor.
I was excited, said we didn't have that C.D.
but could order it in, unalienated suddenly.

She said, "You don't have what I came in for?"
so I said I'd look for it on the computer.
Instead, she glared, yelled at me to "Fork orff,"
a Queen of the Night in an aristocratic huff.

And I couldn't help feeling that myelination
had musically petrified a kind of class isolation:
I'd thought music was meant to do the opposite.

I whistle Sarastro's aria to myself, out-of-tune, ironic.

Note: myelination is the process by which axons in the brain are coated
during infancy and adolescence, solidifying synaptic connections. The
process is more or less complete by late teens.

SHOSTAKOVICH, SYMPHONY 15 IN A MAJOR, OP. 141, 1972

It is just about understandable
how, twenty years later, one thousand miles
away, forty-six-or-so years younger,
a near-boy, sandwiched between cheap-seat trolls
somewhere near Coventry, might find £2
worth of delight in the near-toyshop of
the *allegretto's* malfunctioning fugues,
like demented computers and clockwork
Willie Tells, wound-up towards oblivion;

but less so the *finale*, with its wound-
down Wagners, its ever-grinding Lenin-
gradian-passacaglian earworm
recalled like a past psychosis from an
earlier symphony of attrition;

and least of all, how can a near-boy in
Coventry, who has never stared through those
inch-thick specs at the fires of '41,
the starved lurking for cooked meat, never
heard Zhdanov's decrees, harsh as night-raps on
the door, never so much as lived through some-
one else's death, how is it that this boy
cries in F minor with the *adagio*,
with its brass-chorale-gone-wrong, its cello
solo, tessitura wide as grief, its
mock-Mahlerian dead march pared down to
the very trom-*bones*, its Terror-ridden climax,
its uncelestial celeste near the close?

It should all be as impenetrable
as the Iron Curtain, but the celeste
seems to chime with an inside-vibraphone,
as if a pre-echo – not genetic
nor Jungian, but Shostakovichian –
were ready-made for us all, awaiting
revelation by an outside music,

sometimes, as here, in glimpses, sometimes in
whole life-spans, like an archaeologist
painstakingly unconvering a long-
hidden musical mosaic, or like
a set of variations in which the theme
is revealed only gradually
and finally collapses into an
infinite string chord and a clatter of

percussion.

MAVZOLÉY LÉNINA

Your cadaver was warmer than our houses
and in your baths you didn't just have running water,
oh no, but balsam too, of glycerine, quinine chloride,
potassium acetate, even alcohol. You decadent you.

No leveller, Death and the Committee for Immortalisation
bourgeoisified you, with facials of phenol, hydrogen peroxide,
till you looked better than some of us living Muscovites
during Yezhovshchina, twiddling dead thumbs in crystal casket.

You ran away in '41 and the German invasion
only to shuffle back afterward, unshamefaced.
It was twenty years too late to shoot you for desertion.

SECHS KLEINE KLAVIERSTÜCKE, OP. 19, NO.6

mit sehr zartem Ausdruck

– Arnold Schoenberg's direction in score

Here is Mahler's musical postmortem,
his 4/4 dirges laid out, *Sehr Langsam*,
barely twitching under coroner's scalpel,

reflex-recalling two chords, funeral bells
clanging on Liechtensteinstrasse
which the corpse once told you to set,

and *pianissimo* pre-reminiscences
of *les adieux* sighs at the Ninth's opening,
a symphony cut down to bone

DMITRI SHOSTAKOVICH, ADAGIO-FINALE 'IN MEMORY OF BEETHOVEN,' FROM SONATA FOR VIOLA AND PIANO, OP. 147

Moonlight has been deported
to an Arctic Norilsk or Vorkuta
Rellstab's lake frozen over

surrounded by barbed-wire ostinati
in the wrong time   wrong key
shivering fourths   arthritic fifths

dotted-quaver-semi-quaver
melody glaciated
beneath moonlit surface

Note: Ludwig Rellstab was the music critic who is credited with coining the nickname *Moonlight* for Beethoven's Piano Sonata no. 14 in C-sharp Minor, Op. 27 no. 2, having compared the first movement to the reflection of moonlight on Lake Lucerne.

GYÖRGY LIGETI, POÈME SYMPHONIQUE FOR 100 METRONOMES

... through which, like distant phantoms, appear familiar shadows ...

– Alfred Schnittke on Ligeti

at first it seems just that
one hundred inverted pendulums
miasmatic-melismatic noise

but sometimes micropolyphonic
clouds break with memories
downpours of hailstones

washing away utopian unisons
probably aural illusions
to *bruits mécanique* again

or maybe a marching downwards
all at different crotchets a minute
jackboots to forced labour camps

or deported to a Polish field
where one by one all metronomes
wind down
                    are stilled

VALENTIN SILVESTROV, FIFTH SYMPHONY

I do not write new music. My music is a response to and an echo of what
already exists.

– Silvestrov

The *Postsinfonia* has dementia

cannot piece itself together

from the eschatophonia

piano bass tremolos
flute and harp arpeggios
trombone soliloquies

muttering dissonances
to itself   lost in sequences
of incontinent tics

while melodic codas
from past *Adagiettos*
are half-remembered

and then

MOZART'S CLARINET SEXTET

On stage: Mozart, clarinet, four strings,
next to me: a sozzled hiss-humming
counterpoint of gin, tears and wee:
"Thatsh Beethovensh *Ode to Joy*, that ish."

"No it's not," shushed and shushing back,
the hiss-hum slumps forward on her knees:
"You and me, we're on a promish tonight,"
to a row of husbands, all sober suddenly,

whose postured wives seem transfixed
by an *Allegro* they can only half-hear
willing a periwigged bouncer into being,
conjured from their clenched handbags.

Unbouncered and ignored, hiss-hum sulks:
"You can all go fuck yourshelvesh then."
Back on chair, she's full of nods and nudges:
"Thatsh Beethovensh *Ode to Joy*, that ish."

"No it's not," someone shushes again,
but I begin to dream it's she who's right:
as the hiss-hum percolates the music,
strange how concordantly her descant fits,

drunkenly travelling back and forth in time,
entwining Mozart and a public desperation
with joyful Beethoven,
                              and you never know:
maybe she's right about the husbands too.

EARWORM

A Love Poem

First those *flauti* triplets – then,

looping over and over again,
O terra, addio; addio valle di pianti,

a repetunitis *ad infinitum,*
sogno di gaudio che in dolor svanì …

and nothing can rid me of the *ohrwurm,*
a noi si schiude il cielo e l'alme erranti,

neuronally condemned to G-flat major,
volano al raggio dell'eterno dì:

> and entombed in my synapses,
> voice in voice with Radamès,
> Aïda is still singing and dying,
> forever dying and loving,
> *O terra, addio; addio valle di pianti,*

while offstage, some chorus is intoning,
Immenso Fthà, noi t'invochiam,

now *piano,* now *pianissimio,*
now *pianissississimo,*

and now gone

ON HEARING GLENN GOULD PLAY THE FIRST NINE BARS OF J. S. BACH'S PRAELUDIUM 8, BWV 853/1, FROM THE WELL-TEMPERED CLAVIER, PART I

20th March 2003. For Sam.

And 'mid this tumult Kubla heard from far
Ancestral voices prophesying war...

– Samuel Taylor Coleridge

E-flat minor, 3/2 signature, *sarabande*-ish rhythm,
three tonic chords, strum-*staccato*ed minims,
with *cantabile* treble soaring away from the beat,
simple soprano threnody soon shape-shifting
to arabesques of grief: B-flat, dotted-crotchet rest,
quaver B-flat, dotted-crotchet E-flat, quaver G-flat

to bar two, A-flat minor minims, second inversion,
treble in sequence: C, quavers E, A, C, all flats,
then first shock, as tonic is wormed with accidentals –
Bach showing what new temperaments could do
not just for compromised consonances but
dissonances too, now right-wrong, not wrong-right:

E-flat minim descending to D-natural, F, A-flat,
treble D-natural, resolved next bar on E-flat minor,
but not for long, never for long, as treble leaps up
to G-flat atop broken tonic chord, destabilised
in first inversion, baritone lamenting downwards
to B-flat, with G-flat major chord piled above,

but the major collapses as soon as it is stated
with flattened F in the treble, descending again
to C-flat major, flip-side of B, well-tempered keys
shaky, enharmonically quantum-wavering,
just as the major of next bar's brittle E-flat
crumbles to dust at one touch and treble slips

first into A-flat minor, then F minor dimished,
high C-flat casting a shadow down to bass D –
as early as this, tempered tonality losing footing
among diminished chords, tritones grinding
rocks into chromaticisms, each modulation
a slip-sliding towards modernity's scree,

a mudslide restrained only by old *sarabande* steps,
insistent even at *fortissimo*, holding dodecaphony
back for two centuries yet.
                                        Or not: for suddenly
bursting in my room is a small Person of Porlock
and News: a tritone above, his trebles of laughter,
wrong-right minims below, a diminished-chord future.

SEID NÜCHTERN UND WACHET

I set down a beautiful chord on paper – and suddenly it rusts.

– Alfred Schnittke

Torn to pieces by G minor tango
for chorus, orchestra, Satanic contralto,
where Leverkühn's inverted *Ode to Joy*
meets Schnittke's 'negative passion,'
Faustus is smeared across bedroom,
his brain flung against wall,
limbs quivering in dung-heap,
blood, eyes, teeth on the floor

because Faustus, like so many of us,
realised only when it was too late
that hypocritical Mephistopheles
was mere Puccinian double-cross
and he'd been demonically misled
by contralto and counter-tenor's duet,
their two-faced tonality no more
than seductive G minor snare.
He should have listened to the orchestra
with its truth-telling dissonances instead.

JOY

After Oliver Sacks, *Musicophilia*

At sixty, she woke into a non-stop *Ode to Joy*
and couldn't switch off these L.P.-ish hallucinations,
playing at the wrong r.p.m.s, squeaking like a toy,
or yawningly slow, tired from incessant celebrations.

Beethoven stalked her like Pink Panther's cloud
to Post Office, hairdresser's, on the phone,
her nerve-deafness, once so quiet, now loud,
filled with *O Freunde, nicht diese Töne!*

G.P.s and consultants gave her E.E.G.s, M.R.I.s
that showed blossomings in the basal ganglia
up to the thalamocortical systems, musical lies
scored for chorus and full orchestra.

They put her on gabapentin, risperidone,
checked for cerebral aneurysms,
gave her quetiapine, prednisone,
an analyst tried therapy for narcissism,

but nothing worked, and she felt stampeded
by pressing Brotherhood, drunk from Nature's wine,
recitatived, *presto*ed and *allegro energico*ed
into submission and marched into line.

Forced to ear-drink at the *Brüsten der Natur*,
she unremembered nursing long ago
as a young girl: "You're so mature,"
they'd said, but life had never felt so slow

before or after, when she's tried returning
to college and its choir – no longer wanted:
"You'll need time for grieving not learning,"
they'd said, meaning: forget life, get husbanded,

have another. But she'd thought she hadn't
liked the first, till too late, Beethoven-haunted,
Joy's timpani seemed more like a mallet,
the trumpets like tannoys, feedback-distorted;

and, as time went on, the ear assaults shortened,
no longer whole recitatives or verses, and soon
all that was left was *Tochter* and *Götterfunken*,
those soprano *A*s, over and over again.

Still the music never reached its end,
the coda and *A*s stretching to eternity,
as with Schumann, who was maddened
by that note, sirened by Angels into lunacy,

or those endless *A*s in Shostakovich Five:
"You will rejoice, you will rejoice, you will rejoice,"
beating you with a Joy-stick till you're barely alive,
and you know you do not have a choice.

FEAR OF MUSIC

After Oliver Sacks, *Musicophilia*

        – and thus in an orchestra
of dissonantly fuguing synapses
music wreaked its neurological revenge
on the critic,

        making an example
of poor musicoleptic Nikonov,
tenor-seized one Meyerbeer evening
in St. Petersburg's Imperial
and temporal lobe

        by Le Prophète's
ecstasies with twitching eye,
symphonic headache, then deafening
unconsciousness.

        Later, brass-convulsed
through the motor cortex by automatisms
of street-marching bands
and ultimately Wagnerised into a
grand mal chaos –

        whereby, in his very neurons,
every sound, from Meyerbeer to Wagner to
the military, was epileptically equalised
by similar symptoms, no doubt
to Wagner's disgust –

Nikonov found his critical
faculty, understood as differentiation
and hierarchization, physiologically
short-circuited by all rhythmical
and melodic fits alike.

SLEEPWALKING

Transformed into someone else's ghost,
I don't even remember the screaming
of that 2 a.m. incident in Aberystwyth
when, after a day's stationery stock-taking,
I glided into the room where my manager
was nakedly taking stock with his wife,
fingers frantically searching one another,
left hand mistrusting right and vice versa:
Where are the 83p cards? I murmured.

Another post-pub night I drunk-dreamt
into my parents' room, mistaking for the toilet
their overflowing wastepaper basket.

The Royal Infirmary's sleep specialist
to whom I confessed my parasomnia,
non-REM automatisms, noctural enuresis
seemed unworried (unlike my mother),
didn't diagnose partial-complex seizures,
merely prescribing bells round door and bed,
alarms when slow wave sleep malfunctioned.

But they didn't stop that next time when
you and I somnambulated synchronously
and horizontally,

                    which makes me think
the problem's more with the waking and awake,
and certainly not with us. Everything, my lover,
would be fine if we all were always asleep,
in sync.

            We throw away bells, together.

THINGS NOT TO TALK ABOUT IN ANTE-NATAL CLASSES: A SIMPLE GUIDE FOR FATHERS-TO-BE

Caesareans, bleeding,
bottle-feeding,
pain,

intensive care, depression,
hypertension,
prematurity,

because it's a synonym for pain, poetry,
religion in case one couple is evangelical,
Darwinism and certainly not the Fittest and Survival,
cosmology because everyone'll think you're eccentric,
politics, global economics, sex, race, films, music,

everything else.

If in doubt, sit behind your partner slightly
smiling redundantly, embarrassed mildly
by what your sperm has done.

Afterwards, take your partner by the hand,
help her to the car, close doors, central lock
and chatter together like a pair of puppet-socks
about anything you want.

NUMEROMANIA

For R.

And do you remember how for those miles and miles
of his Seventh Symphony I would walk you up and down,
every step a crotchet: *Allegro moderato, Adagio,
Sehr schnell, Bewegt doch nicht schnell?*

Perched on my shoulder, your three pounds shrieked louder
than an orchestra in E major. You were sometimes *piano*,
sometimes a wild *Scherzo*,

                          as I walked you up and down,
every step a crotchet: *Allegro moderato, Adagio,
Sehr schnell, Bewegt doch nicht schnell.*

And I thought of Bruckner and his counting mania,
flowers on women's dresses, leaves on trees,
notes, bars and phrases, windows in churches
to which he'd otherwise feel compelled to return,
footsteps he'd have to retrace,

                          walking up and down,
every step a crotchet: *Allegro moderato, Adagio,
Sehr schnell, Bewegt doch nicht schnell,*

no-one crying on his shoulder.

URANUS V

...my dear one, thee, my daughter, who
Art ignorant of what thou art.

– Shakespeare, *The Tempest*

Your terrain is a Shakespearean row,
cratered with Alonso, Prospero, Trinculo
squabbling three billion kilometres from Milan,

all now castaways in the wrong plays,
coronae of Arden, Elsinore, Inverness,
regiones of Mantua, Sicilia, Ephesus,
a Birnam Wood-less Dunsinane,

a geological intertext of catastrophes,
cryovolanic eruptions, tectonic uprisings,
canyons, chevrons, *sulci*, Verona *rupes*,
a cataclysmic collage of script-shatterings
pasted back together by gravities,

a motley world of places you wouldn't know,
of other people, father, lover, king, fool:
here you're never your own true self –
that Mirandian self who's much nearer home.

51

THE CRITIC AS BABY

Watching my baby daughter turning
pages of *Lost Puppy Finds a Home*,
patiently, steadily,
as if she were Adenoid Hynkel
spinning the globe,
pointing where to strike next,
reminds me of my father toward the end
turning pages of a TV dinosaur book,
pictures upside-down,
monsters of the Cretaceous inverted,
hanging onto the world by talons,
Hebrew-like, world and history turning backward
from apocalyptic comet to T. Rex to protozoa,
turning, turning, back to world as lava,
then forward again to the end credits –

and it would be all too easy to see
such turning as mechanical echo of forgotten skill,
to see my daughter's turning
as pre-echo of forgetting
before she can even remember,
too easy to criticise
when all we in-betweeners do is the same,
perhaps worse, in our turnings forward, backward,
our atomising *Middlemarch* and Pound,
just as I look up and find my daughter
shredding *Lost Puppy*, Eliot, dinosaurs
into an efflorescence of snowflakes,
an intertextual blizzard,
but with more pleasure,
and perhaps more beauty.

DOLLS' HOUSE

The dolls' house is in a constant state of crisis,
daughter's shrieking head stuck in bay window,
father drunk-collapsed among living-room debris,
headless son dangling from attic feet-down –
"Oh noooo, not again!" – after an earthquake,
mother cowering from ten-foot dog in cellar
who's snarl-woofing among the wreckage
while fire-persons Snow White and Cinderelly
surround them all with Fisher Price sirens,
prophetically pre-empting inevitable fires.

Only grandma sits still on her attic chair,
ignoring grandson's upturned soles, alone
untouched by natural disasters,

her thoughts silent, wooden.

TANTALUS-BY-PROXY

On a verandah in Cypriot high summer
my daughter is threatening to eat petals.

> On a sofa ten years ago
> my father keeps threatening the edge.

On a verandah in Cypriot high summer
my daughter keeps toddling to the petunias.

> In a living room ten years ago
> my father keeps shuffling to get up.

On a verandah in Cypriot high summer
I keep putting my wine down, getting up.

> In a living room ten years ago
> I keep groaning from the piano stool.

On a verandah in Cypriot high summer
I keep taking the petals from her hand.

> In a living room ten years ago
> I keep pulling him back: "Stay still."

On a verandah in Cypriot high summer
I sit back down again, sip the wine.

> In a living room ten years ago
> I sit back down again, stroke a discord.

But on a verandah in Cypriot high summer
my daughter is trundling to a flower box.

On a sofa ten years ago
my father keeps threatening the edge ...

... and I know I'll have to put down my wine
or leave the piano stool again, again,

and with inch by painful inch of toddling
and shuffling and edging and threatening

comes that creeping horror
that the precipice of sofa ends
only in the Underworld,
that caring for someone
is Sisyphian in its circularity,
even Tantalusian, or at least
Tantalusian-by-proxy,
the seemingly endless repetition of the
cared-for almost getting the dangerous
or poisonous or self-harmful
thing he or she wants –
to eat rainbow petals,
to escape the safety of a sofa
for a potentially hip-breaking,
            ankle-twisting,
                        nose-shattering
                              floor –

and you the carer are condemned
to be Hades,
forever taking away
what Tantalus thinks
Tantalus wants.

CYPRUS, 2009

... and here, the very sun pants for breath,
its parched tongue lolling over
building sites the colour of bones,
and no-one talks about the weather
because changelessness isn't interesting –
or because changelessnes is a subject which
once started has no ending,

                           like the
incessant building, the country never seeming
finished, houses and their shells
perched like domestic fortifications
so close together that an enemy
would surely be lost in a suburban labyrinth,
wandering endlessly, never finding the
centre,

                 like those masses you sometimes
see on the green line of horizon –
threatening to change the changelessness,
storming through the dust,
rattling the scaffolding,
unearthing the dead,
mobilising old men in ill-fitting caps
forever sat on chairs in shaded corners
not talking about the weather –
but which never close in,
as if they too are lost
in a fortified maze of blue sky.

SONG OF INNOCENCE

A week after your mother
was kidnapped by cancer
we read *Songs of Innocence*
in class

starting with teacher
we each yawned one stanza
lost in unecchoing green
daydreams

until your third turn as reader
fell on 'The Chimney Sweeper':
When my mother died, I was very young,
& so on.

You spoke it like a bored vicar,
or hollow political orator
speechifying from a distance,
unconvinced.

Later I heard the same teacher
discussing poetry with another,
something called 'relevance'
outside class.

Daydreams swagged, weeped,
echoed.

LEAP OF FAITHLESSNESS

For A. and B.

But if I were to tell you that our old
R. E. teacher
               – you know, the one who was
also a tambourine preacher, who
O.H.P.ed us with the Great Flood
(as if coloured in live at the scene)
in which felt-tip dinosaurs missed the bus,
and were drowning, not waving, while
Noah whistled away with his brood
oddly forgetful of creatures so huge,
swept away by this De-Creation,
no doubt because of their capital sins:
Ira, *Fornicatio*, *Vanagloria*, red-meat *Gula*,
and now deluge-desperate *Tristitia* –

would you believe me, turn Darwinian,
if I were to tell you this man was himself
a Tyrannosaur of sin,
who ran off with the sixteen-year-old daughter
of someone else's wife, his lover,
and years later was chucked in jail as keeper
of an un-Church called *City Divas*?

Would you believe all this,
take the leap of faith in reverse,
hold Kierkegaard up to mirrors,
jump back to absurd reality over an abyss
of flailing dinosaurs?

Or would you just think I was taking the piss?

YOU'RE SO VAIN, I BET YOU THINK THIS POEM IS ABOUT YOU

This poem is not about the one true psychopath I have known
(you know who you are – or perhaps more worryingly you don't)
for she or he would not make a good subject for poetry
and as a poet I'm not expected to believe, most probably,
that a person can act without motivation except sadism
that behind his or her eyes, moustache, toothbrush or bushy,
can be a blank black-hole of banality, on the event horizon
of which I once teetered

                       but this poem isn't about him or her.
Instead, it is about the long lawned evenings that Summer
with someone I loved and a bottle of plonk, till birdsong breezes
teetered on the knife-edge of chill.

NEUTRON STAR

I have compacted the dead star of you
to a twenty-kilometre nuclei of neutrons,
where a teaspoon of memories weighs
5×10^{12} kilogrammes

and where the teaspoon itself
is bent downward by gravity
2×10^{11} that of home,

its protons, electrons crushed to neutrons,
like anything else which comes too close,

which is why I have also banished you
at least 5,000 light years along
the Orion-Cygnus arm of my galaxy
where your pulses can only reach me

as distant X-rays.

MARCONI

In those two minutes of wireless silence,
if our late Marchese were to be believed,
an extreme case of hyperacusis
beyond superheterodyne, cat's whisker,
T.R.F., trans-Atlantic coherer receiver
might have aurally resurrected Guglielmo,
re-run his state funeral, heart-attacks,
the *Gran Consiglio del Fascismo,*
endless patent battles, Carpathia, Titanic,

reprised radio's pre-history, an infinitude
of undying telegraphic echoes
where everyone is always still saying
everything they ever said all at once
in an incontinent audio Book of Life
right back to the Sermon on the Mount,
from which we might pick up soundwaves
had we antennae or ears big enough.

But in his dreams our Marchese forgot
the electromagnetic interference round it,
drowning his phonic theophany out
with the sheer whiteness of history's clamour,
all those absurd mishearings *à la* Python,
let alone scratches, coughs, farts and yawns –
that, *pace* Larkin, what may survive of us

        is mere noise.

MYSTERIUM COSMOGRAPHICUM

To Frederick, Duke of Württemberg, 25th February 1596.

Your Grace,
          My Natural Sovereign,

described herein, as you requested,
is my remarkable recipe for the Universe,
polyhedra of which should be constructed
by different craftsmen, so that the perfect
geometry of Platonic solids with five orbits
remains secret:
                              starting-point is Earth's orbit
figured as hemisphere in dodecahedron,
inscribed in Mars's orbit inside tetrahedron,
the circle surrounding which is Jupiter,
inscribed in a cube encircled by outer
casing, the circumgyration of Saturn;
                                        in turn,
Earth's circuit encloses icosahedron,
then hemisphere for Venus, octahedron,
inside of which is the orbit of Mercury,
with our glorious Sun, decorated tastefully,
centred, as Copernicus well knew it to be.

And from the Sun, Moon and planets,
Your Grace will be pleased to hear,
issue seven Solar System drinks,
aether in each planetary hemisphere
channelled through concealed pipes
to Saturn's rim and convenient taps,
Venus dispensing mead, Mercury brandy,
Mars vermouth, Sun *Aqua vitae*,

Moon water, Jupiter a fresh white wine,
Saturn a bad-beer-trap to ridicule ignorance
of those who, unlike yourself, know nothing of science
or alcohol.
                    And the totality of this Universe
will be no more than an ell in diameter,
with diamonds for Saturn, jacinth for Jupiter,
pearl for the Moon, all orbits and polyhedra,
of course, intricately fashioned in silver,
so Your Grace will own something more glorious
than any Creation bowl of Timaeus
or that overrated ugly Mug of Nestor.

I have built a prototype so you can see
what I describe more clearly;
                                at present, however,
my Universe is made only out of paper.

Your Obedient Servant, Johannes Kepler,
Mathematicus of the Illustrious Estates of Styria.

SN 1054

For Kathy and Helen.

Disputed excerpt from *Vagantes per Mundum, Ecclesiam et Caela*, 11th Century AD, author unknown: free translation into modern English from the Latin original.

It was sunset of the twenty-seventh Calends
of the seventh month of that year of horrors,
the eve following St. Thomas Apostle's Feast
which we had spent well-housed in the Culdee
Monastery at Dunkeld, when Br. Michael & I
climbed a barren prominence known locally
as Dunsinnan, a day southeast from the Monastery,
& which resembled nothing more nor less
than a Scottish Calvary, & there we laid eyes
on what seemed a cross bloody in the heavens
which, in my irreverence, I presumed to be
the Sixth Seal rupturing in the skies
above our very heads,

        for we had heard murmurs
of circumstances from our brethren at Dunkeld
which St. John of Patmos might have foretold,
foremost of which was His departure to Christ's table
of the soul of Our Most Reverend Bishop of Rome
Vicar of Christ, Holy Father Leo IX,
may His memory be sanctified, & also
of an atrocious heresy threatening in the East
to split our Church like bread, so all seemed
afeared at that time of the Last Trump
& Unquenchable Fire,

                              & our guides too
were seized with trembling at the bleeding heavens
& took the red miracle as more worldly omen
of bloodshed for their beloved *Rí Deircc*
to whose service they were travelling
& whose hair is said to be crimson as the hands
of Iscariot,

                    yet Br. Michael, who had spent years
cloistered with the Ptolemaic books, reassured us
that we were mistaken in our diverse presumptions,
that the redness was neither Sixth Seal nor ill omen
but the sandstone of the Monastery from whence
we had journeyed & wherein lay blessed remains
of Saint Columba, who with Christ & Holy Father
were remembering to us Our Lord's Nativity
in St. Matthew & the light followed by Magi
to Herod,

                    & Br. Michael insisted I record the light
in these annals as a sign sent us for good reason
in this particular place, & he told me as his scribe
to record that it glowed in the constellation
known as the Heavenly Bull & he pointed to us
Elnath, Pleiades, Aldebaran, the red light
a finger length northwest of the bull's horn
Zeta Tauri,

                    & Br. Michael reminded us of Job:
'Canst thou bring forth Mazzaroth in his season?'
& he told us that, as it was in the Judge's sign,
the red light showed Our Holy Father had been
accorded such powers posthumously,
to separate with St. Peter souls of heaven

                              65

& earth, & reassure us that all would be well
in temporal as in spiritual realms,

                          & then as if
in consecration of his words the light suddenly
seemed an effulgent benediction on all our faces,
scarletting the night & its shadows, seeming
to move the very hills, the very forests around us,

& all agreed it is good to know that to read the sky
& its signs rightly is always to find comfort.

This is the Word of the Lord. Thanks be to God.